The Museum of Disappearing Sounds

Zoë Skoulding
The Museum of Disappearing Sounds

SEREN

Seren is the book imprint of
Poetry Wales Press Ltd.
57 Nolton Street, Bridgend, Wales, CF31 3AE
www.serenbooks.com
Facebook: facebook.com/SerenBooks
Twitter: @SerenBooks

The right of Zoë Skoulding to be identified as
the author of this work has been asserted in accordance
with the Copyright, Designs and Patents Act, 1988.

ISBN: 978-1-78172-071-4
ISBN e-book: 978-1-78172-073-8
ISBN Kindle: 978-1-78172-072-1

A CIP record for this title is available from the British Library.

The publisher acknowledges the financial assistance of the Welsh Books Council.

Cover image: Kate MccGwire
'Breathe' 2006 Archival digital print, 90 x 120 cm

Printed in Bembo by Bell and Bain, Glasgow

Author's website: www.zoeskoulding.co.uk

Contents

The Museum for Disappearing Sounds

exhibit 1

in breath a crackle of static
disturbance
      a detuned radio in one lung

drones erase one other
      electricity sings in D
tyres slur across the street

a shoreline just out of sight
         at the base of the skull

exhibit 2

you hold the rise
and decay in its arc
      before dispersal
in wind on the microphone

cough in wave forms
count the layers

but when the light goes quiet
you sleep under air
        roaring
through the tunnel of your throat

exhibit 3

today I'm dripping into forests
                far into sleep
where you can't find me
cannot catalogue the rustle of larch
unpick
        pixel by pixel
the stones under my feet

exhibit 4

in thin vibrations of the phone
a voice shimmers on the end of a line

while outside
                ring dove calls
slip over branches into memory

breath hops and starts
            is this is this is this is this is this
I vanish in lossy compression

birds listen
                come in and drop out

the rhythms that cradle us
turn to an I-you stammer of ringtones
on the nervous system's high whine

exhibit 5

in a frame of silence
                              the spectrum
              shivers into transmission

in a forest of black and white
off-channel   branches
interlace over water   dark
          and interrupted light

the moon is close   closer
or retreating
behind the traffic far off

                    coming and going
accelerates to slow-mo as rhythm
turns to pitch and sinks to drone

Gwydyr Forest

through white trees nothing said
    the edges grow sharper the hills
        farther away with each degree

below freezing under feathered
    water landscapes turn to vapour
        in our mouths clouding the route

you test the surface by stamping this weight of
    our bodies enough to live by measure
        an echo from one side of the lake to

another in summer there are dragonflies
    now heat is something I can't even
        remember we call back to our

outlines scuttle stones across the water
    stacked in lattices of molecules we
        reassemble contact held to breaking

I can do more dangerous things
    just with my eyes or crack the ground
        without even trying we fall

over moss tundra scale shrinks
    to skin print claw track in ice
        that up to this point holds

The Man in the Moone

1.

it's always night before the words and in this
silence something startles out of nowhere
crashes into earth with no-one to look back

or say what a body was before and what has
changed in it as fingernails crescent into moons
to shadow month by turning month

or what is the name of this silence all steely
reflection still waning where the moon
slips away under cover of detectable traces

what it looks like from here is all I can tell you
now it's all push and pull all yes no maybe
all credit and loss all of it passing through

the others I am speaking I am walking I am
eating I am sleeping I am writing only I
could have written this only you will read it

2.

the future was invented with its tense
a shadow falling where our atmospheres are
breath on windows sun scoring lines into skin

a sentence reverses itself between two
pairs of eyes discovering a distance suddenly
exposed in words that run on without stopping

for you to be anything without them
the timbre of the body half sound half
weight as if between us thought were pressure

distributed in music the tension of a
single note everywhere between breaths
holding inside it weight and distance in

gravity as tightrope stutter they row
themselves through air with giant fans and
utter their minds by tunes without words

3.

since the impact event you've carried
strange dust in your throat farther and
farther away the saying and not

being able to the being and saying and not
knowing how to at the limits of a tongue
lost in orbit circling and circling

and burning up starry Laika out there
somewhere as dog dust cold wars racing
through the politics of dream space

it is exactly this far and no farther
the moon eclipsed by the idea of moon
cut out and leaning through the night

a blue that eats away at stones the sky
heavy with it in the distance drifted by a
word shaken loose from border controls

Inventory

tape recorder

reel to reel beginning with
your own voice returning un–
like itself heavier and
thicker in rustles and clicks
of words outside the head where
a life may be erased with
its own sound replaying in
another room relatives
freeze up in the occasion
addressing a future that
doesn't know them or a child
close to mic go on it's like
a telephone but it won't
say anything back hello

colander

cauliflower florets shake
a hollow rattle under
cold water in a sixties
sink raw stalks in the garden
snails and broken glass a drowned
wasp in a turquoise tumbler
drags up a day that hasn't
been invented yet leaking
into steam spaghetti strands
crab apples with shreds of leaf
mould stuck to them blue plastic
faded and brownish through so
much forgetting so many
kitchens so much water rinsed

morris traveller

sunburned legs ripped unstuck from
vinyl seats j-reg in the
democracy of travel
50mph shudders
through oil price hikes and hedgerows
looming foxgloves goats thudding
in the boot straw trailing down
empty lanes futures mushroom
in the wooden window trim
blades of grass and unseen things
first lesson on the airfield
jolts between slabs of concrete
a journey elsewhere at the
same time or squeal of wrong gear

cellar door

asbestos-backed and thudding
shut on dust it is cold and
it is war or there will be
we project and survive with
water canisters for when
the dark will shelter us the
beauty of a word no guard
against the radiant air
for now it's just the work bench
cleaning shoes and skinning hares
in linear time the rasp
in his chest invisible
particles fall from the sound
of a door shut beyond words

singer sewing machine

the hum before the needle
falls or stops snagged on cotton
as the singing starts around
the edges of hems almost
hanging straight but for hidden
glitches every garment an
argument with itself cut
to a pattern but falling
short I wear my own failures
hope on my sleeve the tissue
paper crackles between its
pins over the outline chalked
in a shape cut out of then
by scissors that never stop

enamel casserole

clatter of a lid on blue
and white enamel inside
there's mackerel a small catch
mushroom onion tomato
a child picking endlessly
over the bones brought back from
far out at sea thrashing in
a bucket something alive
catches in the throat after
hours of wind on skin its rush
on the ear diminishing
voices on the shoreline where
the past turns on the tongue and
its chewable emptiness

piano

how to sustain the dark tone
echoing through timber from
pentatonic forests scored
on snow the disappearance
of each sound giving way to
another further inside
the jangled tantrum of wild
keys that open nothing as
pedals thump on felted wood
in the present historic
every string resonates with
a coating of light rust tuned
to a future already
answering its own movement

television

disturbance in the room a
shallow voice takes soundings from
the corner in black and white
treble and hiss insistent
high pitched whine behind the words
bleaching to zero this is
where history flutters under
our eyelids in sleeping screens
events take place or take the
place of events in the air
surrounding us video
killed the radio the stars
are humming quietly in
skies that haven't reached us yet

Ô

while tones of planets descend
in scales as if thought were pitch
not picture but single note

while in the river's light spots
a train passing overhead
still in the rush of brakes you

while with tightening of the throat
air passes through zero cries
circumflex and gutteral

while the moon's full of lost things
migrating birds unanswered
prayers keys emails of the dead

while re-engraved with its own
watered silk grainy surface
footage close up then far off

while a body talking to
itself blood and nerves as sleep
rises through ears and water

while two heads crossed in the glass
a train passing from one ear
to another right to left

while this story's full of holes
in the edges of the space
you filled very slowly I

Variants on a Polish Fragment

after Julia Fiedorczuk

this is glass this is *szkła* or *szkło* depending on where
it catches the light and I can't see anything through it
only hear the rasp of broken bottles
swept across a beach where I'm walking
towards you with bare feet in this variant
salt air wears the edges smooth

words are sharp against the town's low roar
but blur your ears and traffic turns tidal every step
leaves a white wave of salt on my shoes
in *wody wielkie* in vast waters I could
drown in the undertow of any language
in this variant it would make no difference

if green's as green as *zieleń* I am walking through it
scent of cut grass on the rubbish tip
overhang of leaves dripping on the pavement
in this variant I'm spit and shadow ticking inches
over earth's impossible face this is how close I am
when shades of meaning grow luminous

in this variant I'm split in glass with one face
to the street and one tilted into planes where colours
fold back in silence the smell of rain
vanishes in the future there is no drizzle only
specks of scattered shine across a lens
in this variant you can't hear me coming

it's a city that asks questions, gives no answers

after Sigurbjörg Þrastardóttir

we may still cry in taxis
          though behind the window
it's not winter the electricity
          grids are humming
there has never been a word
          for crossfire in this language
shuffle the deck which one
          will you choose how will you
construct a house of cards
          so the stones won't fall
below the currency the city
          has thirteen hearts and none of them
is beating the circulation
          gone you play your hand
in this uncertain state
          it was not a heart attack
when he fell his ear
          pressed to the ground for
six-month-old information
          or digital toxic waste
grassed over the carbon cost
          of data cold enough to handle
she signs five times to say yes
          this is the whole truth all of it

In Search of Lost Time

I

After you've lost, searched, and come up empty,
you move on. For a long time I used to go to bed early
but the system clock is not accurate. You have
two options: one is to install timesynch software
but that won't hold for very long, so why not work on
punctuality yourself? I replaced the battery and that
seemed to do the trick. In all this gorgeous atmosphere
I dress in black every day, adding new features
where possible. Imagine having permanent jet lag
when legal professionals capture elusive billable time,
such as that spent giving reasons and dates, plus
sunrise and sunset in several hundred cities.

II

In real-time station departure I am unsuccessful in
retaining possession of the number of days, which do not
include the day of injury or day of return. No earlier
geared mechanism of any sort has ever been found:
it's always under construction, always under the burden
of unreliable data, but countdown clocks would show
how long this misery could last. A China lost in time
due to migraine symptoms swallows hours and hours.
Who can you turn to when times are flying out of joint?
Playing catch-up, she's fully engaged and ready to lead
the archaeological expedition that disappears and reawakens
elsewhere, the system behaving well during a finite period.

III

He would suddenly become aware that he could not
remember even time-lapse cameras recording glaciers.
A reasonable attempt will be made to replace time lost
but there is no magic form. Ask your doctor to complete
a press release pertaining to cloud estimates after earthquakes.
How can one hold joy and grief in the mind at the same time?
Blame advertising slowdown, or the growing literature
on the economics of migraine. Little is known about
why subjective time loss occurs after a novel experience
but mice allowed to sleep after being trained help you
shed flab in a jiffy. Between accident and absence
the world had changed into something unrecognizable.

Wingprint

the colour of power hanging in the air
                    is a word for sun on warm stone
made transparent

as sky and trees
            repeat leaves in flame
                        on the other side a flight path

where finches throw their outlines
                        wings etch themselves on windows

in the stun of what stops them
an identified span
of feather grease and dust

                                        a curve of passageways
glazed over a bird
                    flies in
                                lost in exits
            and entrances   a tongue silent
                        behind a mouth that moves through glass

when the door is locked it is alarmed
                            somewhere between G4 and E7
or what I know and and how it's different from X

a restless wish for   what can't be googled
            and if so is it knowledge
                                    or the lost keys
that apple F won't retrieve

Orion

stars stream information out of date
before it gets here sky fills half
the field of vision he replays his son's
steps or his own or chewing gum
stuck in the pocket of secondhand jeans
in 1978 an embroidery knotting the past
in place or fraying ways through
what time cuts up as the story cuts
across the short edge of the field drawing
forgotten paths into itself the lines

of memory static in blood and baying
there's a mess of crushed feathers
damp behind the door creaking open
over stone the scent of infrastructures
east to west now an owl circles
soil shifts from clay to sand the rattle
of his father's lungs as something's torn
apart on my tongue we grow fat
on history bright bodies in playback
move before you can see them

Ex Situ

We shall shortly be arriving into
                    scabious across the track
derailment ahead
                    still in sunlight

passengers
          drowse through time
          scarce as tortoiseshell
butterflies or the names of them
          falling away   brown
                              with red wingtips

language spattered all over
          his t-shirt   soluble aspirin
dislocates a voice
                    into each stop

a long delay of sleep
          translated into fields
low murmur of mobile
                    phones inside
                    miles and the clouds   roll along
          Penrith Carlisle Crewe

a destination on his sleeve
                    look in thy heart
                    at template on template

as places merge and we
                    arrive into and continue on

From Here

I

what I can hold in the eye breaks

at the edges a cluster of paths a zebra

crossing to the other side of the road side-

walks becoming pavements a shadow

pulled across continents the signs point

in all directions at once down

there in the windblown circumference

of light you carry history from a

to b in planetary drifts across a lens

II

you walk at the edge of land traffic

turning in swathes of sea

that I can't hear from up

here where the glass holds me in

place so that I can't fall into

violet pools under your feet or

out into flightpaths where the sky

a sudden mass of cloud holds

steady you could fall up into it

III

a perforated surface opens down

on every hair every sparrow every

shadow falling in parabolas

every word every world is its own

hidden footfall crosses light

the ground aslant where

walkers sleep along the lines of

habit scored in ink barely

reading the grid one instant to

IV

another where a corridor streams

back to the eye in red the days

marked out in verticals while

absent bodies pulse in shapes

they passed through at the edge of

colour in the corner of an eye

descending walls run into

thoughts replaced by moving images

walk this way and I disappear

V

in years of hours and hours of years

bricks disintegrate the lights on red

where the road folds over I tie

myself in knots trying to see how

the standstill image might lay

everything side by side in static

histories that never happen here

where the lights on continuous loop

flicker into shadow scuff marks vapour trails

VI

under the stones the minutes

scratch away in seconds and nothing

stays when you look a second

time on a curve of thought spiralling

into where I might be written a moment ago

there were futures in bricks

as the ground opens up only the sky's

unchanged in the roughened surface global

weather patterns notwithstanding

VII

our faces scrunch against the sun

in the torn edges summer

berry-stained where birds fly

overhead in strict formation crossing

wet ground as colour seeps over

and into living things where they

begin an arc of movement from

hatching to blur whole continents

do not contain them

VIII

territorial integrity softens into rain

as things get cloudy under

cold fronts of diplomatic pressure

I signed on the dotted line and became

another autumn falling through

copper and bronze the blue winds

in our mouths a scale of connections

balanced at street level

from a storm to a single drop

IX

in our mouths beyond human

beyond habitation the winds

in a circle of eyes on the liquid

surface of social contact

translucent bodies where place

comes through in washes

beyond the city lilac far

off mountains water in the rough

fur of dogs their open mouths and eyes

X

on the tip of your tongue another

word for it that won't settle

under cloud of a half-known

language the tip of ice melts

on the page in the friction of

asphalt under shoes chewing gum

stains map islands corresponding

to nothing elsewhere but better

to know this than nothing

XI

the global falls open early one morning

as if the real and virtual worlds

were different spheres as if the stride

of boots across the street

were not in time with anthems

of nations warping on the car stereo

in the other world its clouds of ink

gather in thumbprints where

each line is your next move

XII

the search engine split

your name into flood victim film

star doctor on four continents we passed each

other in the street a collision

or collusion in air currencies

magnified in cross-section the lens

smudged by speed you were here

a second ago both feet on the ground

flipped over in the sphere of an eye

Gropers

by glym-stick gropers fall in darkman
pike a series of minute perceptions up and down
the dancers of home-bred treachery

through the maunders or meanders of matter
stow your whids and keep one ogle open

in the peeper conglomerations of dust
gather every time you wink your glaziers
as if through a slit in shadows

a flicker snapt as wonderful prediction
rises above a folded glymmer

no longer sees but reads rags twisted
into ropes to bind us in the city's dis-
ordered labyrinth touted through the wicker

History

The poem lying in a suitcase on the fourth floor
describes the attic as a head with closed eyes,

a ship of creaking boards with trunks
adrift in elsewhere, halfway across the sea,

each box still packed with objects reassembled
as signs growing cold: envelopes like folded wings,

ostrich eggs, lies and invitations, letters,
dresses of dead aunts all locked in

but ready to leave on the first breath
out of there. Line by line it tracks

glances scattered in the street below,
roofs sloping this way and that, heads and

tails of coins clinking in a pocket, wind
under the eaves — restlessly, as if a gust of air

could blow it into the dust of this page.

Thermophile

Not yet thunder on the rue des Thermopyles
just before the last hot rain of summer.
30 degrees. Green hanging under grey. The passage
narrows where the Greeks outnumbered by the Persians
hold their ground. If you could live anywhere
you like to think you'd live right here. Black
yellowing under green. Hold on for
three whole days.

                    At first glance the sign read
Thermophiles not gates but lovers. Those who
love hot places who wash in hot springs under
falling green who breathe sulphur for oxygen.
70 degrees. How much warmth does it take
to hold out under the green flare of the sky
the gates too hot to touch.

Count down

9.

when underfoot the dust won't
rest where it fell as the ground
trembles becoming nothing
less than itself at each step
down in time out of joint time
being all we have to hold
us together I listen
to the empty corridors
like a skull that could sing once

8.

when a song with no body
but clearly belonging to
someone else keeps returning
what obligations do I
have to the shadows that fall
between the buildings between
a thought and a word between
a word and a tongue moving
across the dust and ashes

7.

when dust keeps returning in
particles of what used to
be solid ground over which
no-one flies any more there
are steps descending into
deep industrial echoes
of what was swept clean away
where the earth has never stopped
falling back in blind faces

6.

when blindness is all that makes
the next step possible in
counting down deeper further
under the dust is music
each word a furious ghost
of its own future descent
descant to scored line out of
time I'm out of time again
here help me please count me in

5.

when I count myself among
crowds in reverberant space
as voices collide with walls
falling through the missed letters
on someone else's tongue I
return as dust as if dust
is an echo as if an
echo is the depth of a
word deserted by a mouth

4.

when the desert whipped into
wind falls as dust covering
skin with finest particles
settling in red who can say
where nomad journeys begin
or solid ground ends in rose
haze on a windscreen distance
diminishes in lost scales
blurs in unmeasured azure

3.

when distances are measured
in days between skin that will
by then have been shed lightly
in particles of dust no
protection against the loss
that's a fact grating against
skin's definition of what
I'd like to think it bounded
against the harm of speaking

2.

when harm is shed lightly as
garments that fall from skin shed
at the centre of dust I
am distracted particles
in all directions cinders
scatter at a moment's edge
the skeleton of a thought
call it life in the stillness
underneath the churning earth

1.

when there's no stillness in thought
or in earth that is scattered
finely on every surface
looking back at you from a
future nobody can see
where is the way down and how
many steps must be counted
as the scored earth turns over
underfoot where dust won't rest

Easy listening

Penmon, Anglesey

well what's the question if
song is an answer as the
familiar keeps repeating in
tomorrow rasping over pitted

salt white stones here on the
shore leaning landward
behind the bell that rang
again just when you had

forgotten its interval
flat clouds shadow the sea
facilitate peripheral listening
not ruffling the surface as

écoute your periphery
brushes mine in loud air we
move through as sails catch
the wind and beat out

beginnings that will never
resolve into endings feet slip
in shallow pools each return
of waves hits another

obstacle gathering oil slicks
far away still the same
question repeated in your
skin and blood vessels

Metamorphic

The split slate weathers, lichen colonies
advancing where I stumble in mud, shocked
blood pulsing through limbs, vertical

I tilted in the scent of pine, violent green,
a wood's engine buzz. Up against the wall
my voice comes back not mine: between ear

and stone a rock face turned aside. What's
unintelligible isn't silent, isn't transcendent
blank: it's most of it, including you – this

noise, irresolute as rain, where harmony's
nothing but the hard facts adding up.

Baudelaire

I went underground to   listen to the city
which sounded like my own   body the hammering
of builders somewhere up   above there was a sharp
movement in the shadow   a cat-like flourish then

Baudelaire turned round and   raised one eyebrow I'm so
tired of embracing clouds   he said falling apart
into alexandrines   one of them became his
arm or a giant wing   unbalancing his steps

I took hold of it to   steady myself we walked
counting the seconds in   each echo of our feet
on the flagstones tried to   locate ourselves he drew
a bat from his pocket   stroked it with pointed nails

it rose and flew squeaking   against walls we couldn't
see our words hanging in   the dark air between them
we stumbled the ground un-   even but I found my
footing and let him go   this blank black night he said

is just a screen where you   are barely written you
who well up in my eye   I navigate between
thousands of faces crowds   wash through me I could live
in anyone his voice   was rising even you

but his syllables bounced   back in the slow hollows
under speech that circled   at our edges where they
crumbled in bricks and noise   into which he vanished
as I climbed the worn steps   blinking into the street

Valéry

I went to the cemetery by the sea to find out how time
would sound where white flowers hanging down released
no scent to the midday sun   I followed the signs to

Valéry fast asleep on a blank slab around him a circle
of admiring poets in straw hats who quoted his lines
to him in stumbling unison *où marchent des colombes*

far above the harbour smelling of death and the white
dresses of the singing girls   I walked as far as the distance
folded in his eyelids   I was waiting for him waiting

for him to wake up from a dream that took him far
out over the water in clouds of fish scales over the
sea that was always beginning always beginning

again   insects grated in the dry heat   his eyelashes
flickered and he carried on sleeping not hearing my
footsteps or the voices searching their memories

the true sky watching us change between itself and
our shadows   the wind picked up and his eyes opened
we must try to live he said in this poem that will never

be finished but only abandoned   listen he said don't you
realise how beautiful silence can be   at that point
the poets stopped reciting   there was only wind

Rimbaud

I went out to sea in a small boat   to find the balance
between my ears the waves were full of vowels   long

green tentacles that slipped   around the wrist I trailed
in the water it might have been mine   I couldn't tell

whether the boat was moving   through the milk and stars
or moved through me   the voice I was in was Rimbaud's

a drowned man insisting *je est je est je est*   and all his
others like anemones opening and closing   I is others

passing through   but what if they don't pass what if they
all stay   that means I have to keep moving he mouthed

through static blue   nothing no-one ever leaves I never
leave them   my head full of roads melting patois failed

crusades the flight of silence   now at the helm a fluttering
of cloth around his missing leg   all breeze it was my breath

catching in his throat   I shifted my weight from one side to
the other restlessly the sea now lead   now gold now lead

The Rooms

A room situates the cadence of habit.
Lisa Robertson

Room 321

When entering the room you're forever
in the same place as other rooms forget
themselves
                repeating the distance from door
to bed
        chair to window
                          window to floor
to mirror

        Here you are overcome by
your love of mirrors as the slow movement
underneath the surface becomes your skin

In the force field of possible lives you
take three steps to the centre of the stained
blue carpet

        It's here that everything
is happening twice
                once in the body
and once in the words for it
                    and there's no
escaping that song in your head
                       the one
that was in the room and is now in you

Room 201

When entering the room he's listening for
the two silences
                              the one inside and
the one outside the window
                                        still air
settled over plumbing and the vague
hush of wind or traffic
                              the way they fight
each other in his ear

                              If there is
a third silence in the high-toned hum of
blood
              he's paying no attention

                                        Every
cell sings yesterday
                              behind the slow drowse
of numbers multiplying secretly
at his fingertips

                    Every different room
becomes the same in every sameness changed
where sleep undoes the hook
                                        unlocks the eye
that opens in the wall between us

Room 117

When entering the room or leaving it
the dark leaves nothing of itself behind

Swept heaps of sycamore leaves giddy the
wind with nut scent
                        it's autumn and words are
piling up outside the room

                    Gemütlich
startles the dressing table in a puff
of 4711 cologne
great–grandmother tongue
                            ghost of a ghost of
a ghost out of reach at the back of a
drawer where even the dark doesn't belong

Du bist die Ruh

                Any direction of
language is uncertain in this breeze that
reverberates through my chest
                            shaking lace
curtains and their skeleton tracery

Room 401

When entering the room in a memory
that holds inside it yet another room

inside it another
                    diminishing

another inside that one
                         smaller still

down to the smallest imaginable
cell in the skull
                   which can't be contained in
this passage that's expanding in the glare
of the screen with each line you're trying to write
and haven't finished phrasing yet as the
beginning of the sentence slips away
before you reach the end
                          I'm waiting to
enter your head here where the seconds are
suspended and you're sitting at the desk
by the window while night draws its own blank

Room 204

When entering the room you've already
crossed it in an arc completing itself
without your knowledge

                              Footsteps tick digital
this foot
            that foot with no memory
while the mind sweeps analog through sound waves
bouncing off four walls

                        This was the phrase you
remember
            each note altering the last

this was its cadence falling from major
to minor
            willow over water where birds
chant in broken rivers

                        It seems that you're
addicted to this music however
hard you try not to listen to it

The bird sings with its fingers

                        Twice

                              The bird

sings with its fingers

                  Twice

                  I repeat

Room 207

When entering the room
　　　　　　　　　hesitate

　　　　　　　　　　　　You
mustn't look back but you look back
　　　　　　　　　　　　　which means
you'll be dismembered in the old story
or turned to salt

　　　　　　　　Parts of you are folded
in panels of light that cut across the
bottle on the table

　　　　　　　Starting again
and again
　　　　　reassembles the sequence

Repeat

　　　　　We drink from elliptical rims
while the sun that sinks behind the window
illuminates a note folded in two

All of these things are still happening in
the room
　　　　　which is a page torn from a
notebook
　　　　　no longer addressing itself
to anyone in particular

Room 221

When entering the room I find the day
I couldn't place has settled here

                                   Beyond
the window
                rooftops are whiter than the
sky in this music without memory
the same pattern never coming twice
                              or
blotted out

                It's not exactly snowing
but specks drift in the blur between poses

a photofinish or the beginning
of a gesture repeated in the body
as neurons fire in succession
                        wired
across networks
                one name overlapping
another
            becoming fainter while the
sky is grounded for a moment
                        crumpled

torn in the process and yellowing

Room 35

When entering the room you walk over
to the window but the light's not coming
through

        it falls against brick and blocked exits

this is where nothing holds up

                      Now you find
you are lost in a basement where there's no
exchange only repetition

                hands caught
in waves of a body's falling phrases
where we descend

           mid-way through this life a
tangled wood

       white skin etched against grey

                         Look
at death always in a hurry

           try to
move slowly now

         say this in a language
you only partly understand

            Begin
the beautiful sentence you have chosen
without seeing how it will ever

Room 206

When entering the room I can't help but
look again for someone who's just left it

That's only shadow in the corner and
loose electrical cables gone astray

The sound of voices is a pulse coming
from the cellar as if one of my hearts
were somewhere in the building

                                    The room is

inside the music

                      Under the floorboards
is an ache waiting for a body to
inhabit

              Its tremors remember the
rhythm that beat itself out in the days
in the nights
                 in the days
                         nights
                              days passing
where you are still walking towards the door
and I am walking towards the window

Room 25

When entering the room I asked nothing
from it
       I had no idea what it would
give to me
          take from me

               I gave my skin
to shadows in the crevices of chairs

to the dark behind the door that waited
for my outline to cross it
          and at dawn
the calls of birds I didn't recognise
were addressed to someone else
              someone who
had entered the room the night before and
left it forever

       The furniture was
rearranging itself under my hands
in all the expected phrases
          framing
the answers to questions that had never
been asked
       demands that had never been made

Room 4036

When entering the room bathed in data
streams I flick a switch as glittering squares
cascade down the window from far above
the flyover
                where shapes of workers move
in offices of light and figures glide
over screens in rapid unreadable
patterns

          You enter the room in pixels
now you're breaking up
                 there's nothing more to
say you are leaving but I don't know how
to leave this room
             whose walls have suddenly
expanded

          I roam endlessly over
the chemical scent of new carpet that's
drawing me to the exact location
of what I remember not happening

Room 127

When entering the room I could only
make out the phrases I'd already heard
translating themselves into that moment
where what might have been said had disappeared

I'm just playback
     all pauses and stutters
smoothed out in the dimensions of a room
you're hearing from another room
         voices
uninterruptedly saying nothing

where all that remains is the body's pitch
inside the words and beyond them
        the size
of the words filling the room
       no longer
a voice but the room itself repeating
the evidence tone for tone
      faithfully
erasing every note it remembers

Room 302

When entering the room for one last time
to see if you've left anything behind
you'll find it already remaking its
own emptiness

        In the event of fire
take nothing with you

           In the event of
leaving never turn around to see who's
there behind you

        Dans l'intérêt de tous
gardez votre sang-froid

          Under the bed
the dust has gathered skin and silences
waiting for a day that's been forgotten

Best not to look too closely
              a lost sock

a strand of hair

        If there's such a thing as
freedom it's these others in you
               their cross-
rhythms

      You're still here
          haven't you left yet

Room 131

When entering the room you're holding a
key in your hand
                    a number in your head
that will be gone tomorrow

                            Already
it's too late for the pattern unfolding
through the edges of a music that was
thought
        it was the way we thought
                            the dripping
tap
    rain falling
                a rhythm we never
asked for but fell into
                    never missing
a

    What was the number of yesterday's
room

        This is yesterday's key and today's
is somewhere at the end of a pocket
that opens unfathomably
                    as if
I could reach even the silence clanging
between hangers in the empty wardrobe

Notes

'The Museum for Disappearing Sounds' responds to the question posed by R. Murray Schafer in *The Soundscape: Our Sonic Environment and the Tuning of the World* (1977): "Where are the museums for disappearing sounds?"

'The Man in the Moone' shares a title with Francis Godwin's posthumously-published work of science fiction (1638). His book describes the utopian civilization of 'Lunars', who take advantage of the Moon's low gravity to travel around propelled by fans, and who communicate through a wordless musical language. The last two lines of the second section are taken from Godwin.

'Variants on a Polish Fragment' refers to Julia Fiedorczuk's poem 'Wiersz', while 'it's a city that asks questions, gives no answers' takes its title and first line from the poem 'H and H (und Leipzig)' by Sigurbjörg Þrastardóttir. The poems published here were written as part of a collaborative project with Literature Across Frontiers, documented in *Metropoetica: Women Writing Cities* (Seren, 2013).

'In Search of Lost Time' makes use of search engine results for Proust's title.

'From Here' was written in response to images by Simonetta Moro.

'Gropers' uses criminal slang from *The Canting Academy* by Richard Head (1673).

The epigraph to 'The Rooms' is from *Occasional Work and Seven Walks from the Office of Soft Architecture* by Lisa Robertson (Clear Cut Press, 2003). 'Room 206' adapts a phrase from the architect Lilly Reich, which is quoted in the same book. 'Room 127' is indebted to Alvin Lucier's 'I am sitting in a room' (1969).

Acknowledgements

Thanks to the editors of magazines where some of these poems first appeared: Michael Schmidt at *P.N. Review*; Tony Frazer at *Shearsman*; Patricia McCarthy at *Agenda*; Alex Houen and Adam Piette at *Black Box Manifold*.

Some of the poems have also been included in the following anthologies: *The Canting Academy*, edited by David Annwn (IsPress, 2008); *Infinite Difference: Other Poetry by UK Women Poets*, edited by Carrie Etter (Shearsman, 2010); *Identity Parade*, edited by Roddy Lumsden (Bloodaxe, 2010); *The Ground Aslant: Radical Landscape Poetry*, edited by Harriet Tarlo (Shearsman, 2011); *The Best British Poetry 2012*, edited by Sasha Dugdale (Salt, 2012) and *By the North Sea: An Anthology of Suffolk Poetry*, edited by Aidan Semmens (Shearsman, 2013). Thanks to all those concerned.